EXTREME SPORTS

Written and photographed by David Spurdens

Copyright © 2004 Top That! Publishing plc.

Tangerine
Press

an imprint of
SCHOLASTIC
www.scholastic.com

Scholastic and Tangerine Press and associated logos are trademarks of Scholastic Inc.
Published by Tangerine Press, an imprint of Scholastic Inc., 557 Broadway, New York, NY 10012
0-439-68106-5
Printed and bound in China

Contents

From kite surfing to paragliding, this book takes you on a white-knuckle ride into the dangerous world of extreme sports.

Dangerous

Extreme sports are cool and exciting—they are also very dangerous! So before we start our adventure through the world of extreme sport, a quick word of warning. All of the sports shown in this book are performed by professionals after years of training.

NEVER try any of the tricks shown in this book!

Best of the Best

All the people in this book have spent years fine-tuning their individual skills to be the best in the world, whether on the big waves of Hawaii or snowboarding in the Alps. To be the best, they had to work hard, endlessly traveling to do the sports they love. Whether the sport is skating, BMX, or extreme skiing, each of them is a master of the craft. Here is the

insight into their amazing lives and the stories behind the sports.

David Spurdens, Extreme Sports Photographer.

HORS PISTES
DANGER
AVALANCHE

From gladiatorial combat and glacier hiking to surfing and snowboarding, extreme sports have always played a part in our culture.

Jousting

In medieval times, knights in England practiced a sport called jousting. The sport involved two horsemen galloping towards each other with a long jousting pole and attempting to knock each other off the horse—that's extreme!

Glacier Hiking

In recent years, an ancient European was found frozen in a glacier in Austria. Evidence suggests that he fell down a crevasse while crossing a glacier. Today, glacier trekking is considered so extreme that nobody attempts it alone.

Basic Bungee

The forerunner to bungee jumping was witnessed on Pentecost Island, South Pacific, hundreds of years ago. As a test of manhood men tied vines to their ankles and launched themselves from a platform much like bungee jumpers today.

Nat Young, 55, from Australia, rides the biggest wave of the Quiksilver Masters in Hawaii 2003.

Hawaiian Kings

Started by Hawaiian fishermen hundreds of years ago, surfing is one of the oldest forms of extreme sport. It is now a worldwide sporting phenomenon.

Skiing off a cliff.

Extreme Technology

Most of the sports featured in this book have been invented in the last century. They rely on designs and material technology that has only been available in recent years. From complex parachuting materials to plastics used for boards, a lot is owed to the inventors who made these sports possible.

BASE jumping in the Gorge du Verdon, France.

Extreme Fun

In order to survive in the past, people did things we classify today as extreme sports—from collecting food by surfing and traveling over treacherous terrain, to proving one's worth in society by jousting. Today, we do extreme sports for one reason only—fun! Extreme sports enthusiasts equate fun with an adrenalin rush!

Horse racing on a frozen lake in St. Moritz, Switzerland.

In a blur of acrobatics, skaters leap, skid, slide, flip, and turn themselves and the boards all at top speeds. They seem to defy the laws of physics.

History

Skateboarding is a young sport. It got its start in the 60s, when surfers facing small waves put wheels on their surfboards, and surfed the sidewalks. In the 70s, skaters used drainage channels and slopes around buildings for skateboarding. In the 80s, skateboarding arrived in Europe. Soon skaters began creating their own tricks and stunts.

Skating Styles

Street skating: Skating on streets, curb, benches, handrails, and other elements of urban or suburban landscapes. Vert skating is done on ramps or other vertical surfaces. Halfpipe: A U-shaped ramp of any size, usually with a flat section in the middle. Vert ramp: A half-pipe, at least 8 ft. (2.5 m) tall, with steep sides that are perfectly vertical near the top.

Catching some BIG air!

REMEMBER –
NEVER, EVER TRY
THIS YOURSELF!

Off a vert ramp.

Tricks of the Trade

The fundamental move is the ollie. The ollie allows a skater to hop over objects or onto a curb. They keep their feet on the board by pressing down.

Some other tricks:

Air riding with all four wheels off the ground.

Backside when a skater has his back to the ramp during a trick.

Grind scraping one or both axles on a curb, railing, or other surface.

Big Business

Skateboarding is big business today. The top stars are now able to focus on improving their skills by gaining sponsorship deals with clothing and sports equipment manufacturers. This photo was taken in the Bourg St. Maurice Skate Park, France for a shoe ad.

Surfing is a difficult, but exhilarating sport. Here's how the pros tackle the toughest breaks on the planet.

Way of Life

Surfing your first clean-breaking wave is an amazing feeling. In fact, many people who take up surfing are quickly addicted and change their entire lifestyle to improve their surfing prowess. Great surfers follow the best waves around the world, but the rest of us can find excellent breaks closer to home without too much difficulty.

Even professional surfers wipe out in big waves.

Perfect Wave

About 70 percent of the Earth is covered with water, so it's safe to assume there are always great waves to be surfed. From big wave surfing in Hawaii to the renowned swells off the coasts of Europe, as long as you can get to a beach, you can find great waves!

The Pipeline

One of the world's most famous surf spots is the Pipeline, situated on the north shore of Oahu, Hawaii. The wipeout, below, was taken at the "2002 Pipeline Masters" competition.

It is difficult to be unexcited by the sheer force and magnitude of big waves and the way prosurfers make them look easy!

Six World Champions
1. Six of the world's greatest surfers line up in Hawaii, including Shaun Thompson, Mark Richards, Martin Potter, "Rabbit" Bartholomew, and Tom Curren.

Crowd Pleaser
2. Showing perfect form, this surfer demonstrates how to carve a wave at a round of the surfing world championships. Carving through warm, deep-blue seas is the ultimate thrill for most surfers.

Riding the Face!
3. Speeding ahead of the breaking face, this surfer expresses his joy by trailing his hand in the face of the wave. This is truly surfing at its best!

Longboards

4. Over 9 ft. (2.7 m) long, this ultra-stable, but hard-to-maneuver, longboard is great for impressive tricks such as the "hang ten" (where all of a surfer's toes are off the board).

Surf Style

5. You can catch great waves on just about any beach. Check out this guy "ripping," having his way with the wave.

Crowded Surf Spot

6. Unless you are a pro or among friends, "dropping in" on other surfer's waves is not cool!

Huge Face
1. Huge faces like the one pictured above are common at the Pipeline in Hawaii.

Backdoor in Hawaii
2. Not quite as famous as the Pipeline, "Backdoor" in Hawaii has formidable waves offering some excellent surfing.

Bodyboarding
3. Bodyboards or Boogie boards are an excellent way to get into surfing. Cheap to buy, you catch waves lying on the board and using the sides to steer, as pictured.

Big Wave Weather

Big waves are most common when there is a tropical system over the ocean and high pressure system on the coastline.

Swell

As a result of the tropical system, a swell builds in the ocean, causing huge waves on the coast.

Shell Waves

Reefs and rock shelves such as those at Waimea Bay, Hawaii (below), impede the progress of the water, causing it to rise up into a massive wave.

Big waves, like the one pictured below, have immense power. Beginner surfers should not attempt surfing under these conditions.

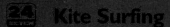

Ripping the face of huge waves, insane jumps, tricks, transitions, wipeouts, and superhuman endurance—that is kite surfing!

Learning to Kite Surf

Picking up the basics of kite surfing is easy, especially if you have board skills. You need to learn how to control the kite. Kite surfing clubs can be found around the world to help you get started.

Beautiful Brighton
Jason Verness catches some air at Brighton Pier, England: "Wave ahead! Power up and touch 35-40 mph (56-64 kmh) before hitting the water on the face of the wave rearing up from the ocean. I whip the kite back above me and go into orbit! Timing is perfect and my flexifoil kite's pulling me higher as it catches the gust. I begin to count airtime— 5 seconds, 6, 7—then the water's coming back up, and I make a perfect touchdown to surf away on the next wave."

Greatly influenced by surfing, sandboarding could actually date back to ancient Egypt and China. And, sand never melts!

The Board

Snowboards influenced the sandboard's design. The base surfaces used on snow did not work as well on sand. Formica used in the boards and special waxes help sandboards accelerate to speeds in excess of 50 mph (80 kmh).

Sliding down the dunes.

Perfect balance is essential for sandboarding.

Where to Sandboard

Sand is very portable and can be found all over the world. Sandboarding is catching on in Australia, Brazil, Chile, France, and Japan, just to name a few spots.

Sandboarding Style

Drags are races between two boarders bombing down a hill, vying for the best time. Slalom races have gates to navigate. Freestyle consists of big air, flips, and turns.

Special wax makes sliding down the dunes as smooth as snowboarding

Snowboarding was pioneered by Jake Burton and Tom Simms in the U.S. Since then, it has taken the world by storm.

Snowboarding requires stamina and speed.

Ask a gym teacher or a trainer for advice on exercises to build up your legs and lower back.

Warming Up
Warming up is very important for snowboarders as you spend a lot of time sitting on lifts, waiting to get to the top of your chosen slope.

Yoga
Yoga is an excellent form of exercise for snowboarders, skateboarders, and surfers as it helps to build strength and increases flexibility.

A mid-air grab.

Simple Exercises
Spread your legs and bend down as far as you can, keeping your legs straight. Now do the same with your legs together. These exercises will stretch your back, leg, and shoulder muscles.

Getting Started
Snowboarding requires stamina, speed, strength, and balance. So before you hit the powder, it is a good idea to work on your fitness level.

Fitness
Cardiovascular exercises, such as running and aerobics, are good ways to build up your fitness level. As with any sport, specific muscles are used in snowboarding.

Turning on a ridge can create amazing powder sprays.

Goofy or Natural?

People have a preference for which foot to place forward on the board. In most boarding sports, this is called "goofy" or "natural." Goofy boarders place the right foot forward, while natural boarders place the left foot forward.

Getting some big air in the Alps.

"Goofy"

Are you a goofy or natural boarder? Lay the board on a flat surface. Place your right foot forward and push off as if riding a scooter. Now, try the same thing with your other foot forward. Which feels more comfortable?

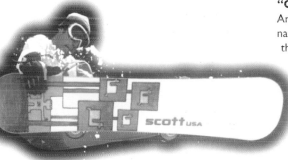

scott USA

DO NOT try this at home!

Styles

The snowboarding style determines how you snowboard, the equipment you need, and where you will ride. As you gain experience, you'll find yourself gravitating toward one of these styles.

Off-piste snowboarding.

Big jumps make you feel like you're flying.

Freeriding

Freeriding is great for beginners. Also, it is the most popular. It's about mastering all terrains with the ride, carving, and jumps. Generally, freeriders like fresh powder. The board is longer with a narrower width, and the rider is positioned toward the back of the board.

Freestyle

Freestyle focuses on the adrenalin rush. It involves doing tricks, on halfpipes and natural objects. The boards are shorter, lighter, and fatter for more maneuverability. Often the tail and tip are the same.

Freecarve

This style focuses on speed with slalom-style turns downhill, similar to skiing. High speeds and powerful turns demand a lot of strength. The boards are longer, narrower, and stiffer for stability.

A boarder trailing his hand in the powder surf-style!

Off-Piste
Off-piste and big
mountain snowboarding
is very dangerous.
Remember, ALWAYS
have a guide who
knows the area. Then
those big powder
turns are yours to take!

"Nothing beats the feeling that you get when you reach the top of a climb."—Mark Hayman, Extreme sports champion.

Ice Climbing

You know you shouldn't be hanging from a 300 ft. (91 m) frozen waterfall by two tiny axe blades and crampons (climbing irons attached to your boots), but you keep going. As with most extreme sports, ice climbing is extremely dangerous. You have to be perfect in your approach to the ice wall, your choice of equipment, your fitness level, and your technical skill. Experience can be gained through instruction.

Climbing a frozen waterfall.

Rock climbing—clinging to a 300 ft. (91 m) sheer cliff face.

Rock Climbing

Rock climbing involves two basic methods: free climbing and aid climbing. A free climber depends on his footwork, ability, skill, and physical strength to pull him or her up the rock face. The equipment used while free climbing is essentially for safety, not for ascending the rock face. Climbing has become so popular that you can go to climbing gyms in most major cities for instruction in this extreme sport.

Facing frostbite, hungry polar bears, and fatigue— Polar trekking is no walk in the park!

Walk of Your Life
If your idea of a good walk is going to the corner store and back, then polar trekking is not for you! You must train hard for a trek in the North Pole to walk on a frozen sea 800 mi. (1,287 km) north of the Arctic Circle. You must have endurance, condition yourself for the temperatures, and have the correct equipment.

Trekking 800 mi. (1,287 km) north of the Arctic Circle.

Extreme Conditions
You must haul all of your equipment and food on sleds across the ice in temperatures of —67°F (–55°C)! Also, the ice can break up and cause you to fall in the freezing Arctic waters. Frostbite is a huge concern, as are polar bears searching for a meal! Extreme dangers abound!

Training for an expedition to the North Pole.

Traveling in a buggy, sometimes on one wheel, at 50 mph with the ground just inches below gets your adrenalin pumping!

Pioneer

Sand yachting was first thought of by Prince Maurice of Nassau in the 16th century. He thought that creating a sail car powered by the sea breezes would surely produce impressive speed across the sand—he was right! It was another 300 years before the idea was resurrected when brothers André and Benjamin Dumont designed the first vehicles to be used in competition in France in 1898.

21st Century

This sport is still going strong, and sand or land yachting still gives an extreme rush. You sit in a plastic frame with a sail above, powered by the wind. You can reach speeds up to 50 mph (80 kmh).

Wheelies

At these high speeds, the sand yacht is frequently up on two wheels and occasionally one! There are no brakes so the direction of the sail and buggy are very important.

Eco-Friendly

It's an environmentally-friendly sport, powered solely by the wind. This is one of the reasons it is becoming so popular.

A sand yachter races to reach the checkered flag.

Acceleration

Acceleration provided by the wind is amazing on breezy days, and lying just a few inches from the ground on your back with your feet outstretched in front of you will guarantee you a thrill. Sand yachts can reach speeds of three times the wind speed, with a recent world record of 116 mph (186 kmh)! There are clubs all over the world with instruction available, so give it a try!

Sand yacht on one wheel!

If you've ever wanted to fly like a bird, try the thrill of hang gliding or paragliding.

Paragliding

Paragliding is a relatively new form of hang gliding. No one knows for sure who invented paragliding, but there are photographs of skydivers using parachutes to fly off of small hills in the late 70s. At about the same time, a handful of climbers in the French Alps began to use skydiving canopies to make exciting descents from the peaks.

Hang gliding and paragliding are becoming very popular.

Thermal updrafts keep you aloft.

Control

The wing is a maneuverable parachute launched by running down a hillside. Pulling or releasing the tension on the control lines controls flight speed and direction. The wings are lightweight and easily carried in a backpack. A student spends a lot of time learning in gentle weather conditions.

A Beautiful Perspective

Two paragliders float beautifully over a lake in France! Extreme sports are practiced in some of the most beautiful areas in the world. This doubles the thrill as you experience top-action sport and breathtaking views at the same time.

Pilot

Almost anyone can fly a hang glider. Since flying depends more on balance and endurance, than on brute strength, woman and men are equally good pilots. Hang gliding instruction has been standardized and most students learn from certified instructors using a thorough, gradual training program. If a person is mature enough to make safety decisions and has good reflexes, they can be a good pilot. Hang gliders can be launched and landed in winds from zero to about 30 mph (48 kmh).

Control

Shifting a pilot's weight controls the glider. Straps connected to the glider frame hold the pilot. By moving side-to-side, forward, or back, the pilot can control turning, direction, and speed.

Lift

The trick to soaring is to figure out where the air is going up (lift) and get there. The common sources of lift are ridge lift (created by wind deflected up off of a surface) and thermal lift (warm air rising).

A rigid-winged hang glider flying high above Lake Annecy, France.

Skiing through fresh powder snow is an amazing feeling. On the steep off-piste slopes it feels like floating down through soft pillows of snow.

Off-piste or Backcountry Skiing

This type of skiing is basically heading off the regular slopes. It is a lot more dangerous than skiing the regular slopes. You should be an expert skier and always have a guide with you.

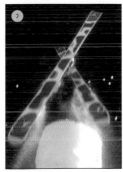

Dangers

One of the biggest threats to an off-piste skier is an avalanche. Steep slopes are susceptible to snow sliding down the face. You must know the danger signs. The snow is a powder, unlike the compacted snow of the ski slopes.

29

Word of Warning

If you plan to ski off-piste always be accompanied by an experienced guide. If you are lucky enough to be there on a good powder day you will remember it forever.

Safety Equipment

As in all extreme sports, safety is important. When skiing off-piste, an avalanche probe is essential in case you get caught. It will be easier to come to your aid or others.

Backpack

It's a good idea to have an avalanche probe, first aid kit, a shovel, water, safety blanket, and a cell phone in your backpack! Many resorts now have cell phone service, so it's always a good idea to carry one, if not for emergencies, then to tell all your friends about the thrill!

Downhill skiing takes immense skill, fast reactions, co-ordination, and plenty of practice!

Downhill skiing is a very fast and dangerous sport. The skiers can reach speeds of more than 90 mph (144 kmh) heading down the mountain, taking corners at nearly the same speed, and are often airborne, sometimes traveling 60 ft. (18 m) or more before landing and continuing down the mountain. Safety wear is minimal with a crash helmet the only protection; the ski suit is designed purely for aerodynamics.

Downhill skiers reach speeds of 90 mph (144 kmh).

Whitewater kayaking is a sport for all ages and lifestyles. Extreme kayaking takes the sport one step further.

Classes

Taking a class from a qualified instructor is very important. Most programs start in a lake or pool. It is best to remove as many distractions as possible while learning the basics. Basics include learning how to get out when upside down, forward, backward, and sweep (turning) strokes, and keeping the kayak from going over.

Wearing a lifejacket, helmet and clothing to protect you from the elements is essential when kayaking.

 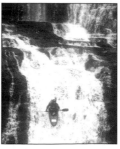

Shaun Baker drops a 60 ft. (18 m) waterfall.

Safety

Wearing a lifejacket, dressing for the water temperature, having good floatation, and kayaking with a part of an experienced group are some basic safety guidelines any program should show you.

Extreme Experience

"I progressed to the violent whitewater of the big weirs on the River Thames. Then by fourteen onto expeditions—the longest being 700 mi. (1,127 km) of sea and whitewater, over $2\frac{1}{2}$ months. The allure of enormous waterfalls began to bite, and I was drawn to a waterfall in Wales that was 50 ft. (15 m) of pure freefall and gave me a new Guinness World Record."—Shaun Baker is the world's premier extreme kayaker.

Shaun Baker kayaking down a water dam!

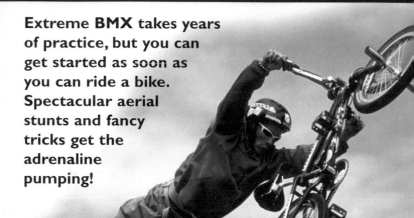

Extreme **BMX** takes years of practice, but you can get started as soon as you can ride a bike. Spectacular aerial stunts and fancy tricks get the adrenaline pumping!

Styles
There are three different styles of BMX:

1. Vert riders take after skateboarders, and do tricks in and out of the halfpipe. Pegs, a detangler, and a front brake are used for vert riding.

2. Dirt track riding consists of racing around a track of jumps and bumps. Dirt riders do not use any kind of special equipment except for safety.

3. Freestyle riding is broken down into two different areas, flatland and street. These riders do tricks revolving around different ways of riding a bike. Pegs, a detangler, and both brakes are a necessity. Some tricks are called bar spins, endos, rocket airs, grinds, and tabletops. Be prepared for a few spills, as you learn these tricks, and don't forget the safety equipment.

Riding ramps, better known as vert (as in vertical), is the most extreme part of park or street riding.

In the Beginning

BMX got started in the early 70s when neighborhood kids wanted to perform stunts like their favorite motocross heroes. They modified their Schwinn Stingrays to ride in lots across Southern California. If you are old enough to ride a bike, you can race BMX! This sport is for everyone!

Safety Equipment

It is basically a safe sport, and injuries occur less often than in many other sports. To help keep BMX thrilling yet safe, you should wear:

* A helmet with a jofa (mouth protection)
* Long pants
* Long sleeve shirt
* Tennis shoes
* Socks, elbow pads, gloves,

Getting big air on a halfpipe

Backflip

In a backflip, rider and bike do a complete somersault before coming back down on the ramp. You need a lot of air and a lot of strength to pull this trick off. Needless to say, it's extremely dangerous and only for the pros.

Corkscrew

The corkscrew is based on the snowboarding trick of the same name. It is very exciting to watch, but extremely difficult to do. A favorite trick of professional freestyler Dave Mirra, the corkscrew refers to any very fast and tight rotation performed off-axis.

Barspin

The barspin involves spinning the bars around when the bike is in the air. The rider has to grip the seat with his thigh and then spin the bars as quickly as possible. It's important to grab the bars before the bike lands!

Barspin

37

Imagine racing down a mountain at breakneck speeds with trees passing you on all sides. Now, that is extreme!

History

Mountain biking began in North America in the early 1970s as a pastime. Soon, two areas of the sport sprang up: downhill and cross country. Downhill is considered the extreme sport, because it is more dangerous and exciting. Downhill biking can range on a variety of terrain, from steep slopes to biking on snow. Snow biking is very extreme, but you should not learn mountain biking on snow.

A mountain bike for downhill is much different to your everyday bike. Downhill bikes sacrifice a lightweight frame for sturdiness. They have full suspension for more traction and control. Disc brakes are very important. It's a matter of life and death.

Riding Tips

1. Keep your weight distributed over both wheels to help with traction.

2. Your handlebars should be between 2-4 in. (5-10 cm) lower than your saddle.

3. Keep your head up and looking ahead for obstacles.

4. Keep your arms bent to absorb shock.

5. Keep the ball of your foot centered over the pedal axle.

Safety First

Mountain biking is a thrilling sport. However, the potential for injury is high—falling from a big air jump or colliding with a tree can be very painful. Bikers wear a lot of safety clothing to minimize the risk of injury, like a helmet and gloves.

The Essentials

A strong bike is a must for extreme mountain biking. But you must be healthy too. Start out slow by conditioning your legs and upper body. Running will increase your strength and stamina. Expect to feel muscle burn, but as you become fit that goes away.

A mountain biker competing in full safety gear.

Big Rushes

"When I was launching the avalanche barrier out in France, the drop was huge, so the fall seemed to take forever, but it was one of the biggest rushes I've ever had."—Rob Weaver, extreme mountain biker.

REMEMBER—
NEVER, EVER TRY
THIS YOURSELF!

Bungee Jumping was invented by the people of the Pentecost Island in the South Pacific.

Modern-day Bungee Jumping

First witnessed in the Pentecost Island in the South Pacific, bungee jumping was originally used as a rite of passage into manhood. It was brought into the 20th century, with elastic as opposed to vines, by four members of a dangerous sports club, who plunged over the 250 ft. (76 m) Clifton Suspension Bridge in Bristol, UK, in the 1970s.

Open to All

No training is required, bungee jumping is an accessible extreme sport. During the summer months, bungee jump cranes pop up all over the world. For a fee, you can experience the thrill of dropping 100 ft. (30 m) suspended by a piece of elastic and bouncing back up again.

REMEMBER—
NEVER, EVER TRY
THIS YOURSELF!

Age restrictions apply for those wishing to try an organized bungee jump.

Strictly for professional stuntmen, you can't get more extreme than cliff jumping. Whatever you do—don't try this yourself!

The Jump

Cliff jumping is standing on the edge of a cliff and jumping off, usually into water. You can jump from 2 ft. (0.5 m) to 80 ft. (24 m) or more above the water.

Planning

Each jump needs to be planned to the last detail, taking into account the tides, wind gusts, depth of the water, and the cliff face.

Blind Faith

When a stuntman performs a cliff jump, her or she is often unable to see where to land.

REMEMBER— NEVER, EVER TRY THIS YOURSELF!

BASE stands for "Building, Antennae, Span, and Earth." Strictly for stuntmen, BASE jumping is the most extreme sport in the world.

What is it?

BASE jumping consists of jumping from a fixed site (building, antennae, span, or earth) with a parachute on the jumper's back. The chute is either thrown out from the jumper's hand or tied to the structure and it then unfurls as the jumper falls through the air.

Deadly Pursuit

If the chute does not open the jumper is in serious trouble and may well be seriously injured or killed. This makes BASE jumping the most dangerous of all extreme sports.

Eiffel Extravaganza

Gary Connery is the man (pictured right) jumping through the center of the Eiffel Tower in Paris. The weather that day was terrible with 25 mph (40 kmh) winds, rain, and sleet being blown through the tower.

The Big Jump

Gary jumped out from the Eiffel Tower and his chute snapped open. As he came below the legs of the tower he was blasted out of the side by the wind. He hit the road, just missing all the traffic. After a week in hospital with broken ribs, Gary was sent home.

How It Started

Carl Boenish is known as the father of modern BASE. In the late 1970s, he was the first to use modern gear and modern freefall techniques to jump from a fixed object.

Gary Connery's landing in the Paris traffic caused several broken ribs, resulting in a short stay in hospital.

Left: BASE jumping New River Gorge Bridge, West Virginia.

Gorge Du Verdon
While on a white-water rafting photoshoot in the Gorge du Verdon in France, I came across Ben, a French fireman, who was going to BASE jump into the gorge. As he made his way around the edge of the rock, and jumped out and started his freefall, we held our breath. His chute opened and we all breathed a sigh of relief. Ben floated safely to the valley below.

BASE jumping the Gorge du Verdon.

Photographing extreme sports is just as difficult as the sport itself. Taking photos of powerboating while strapped to a helicopter is a rush.

Extreme Photography

Capturing these death-defying feats is not easy. Taking this type of photograph should qualify as an extreme sport in its own right!

Power Boating

As the helicopter takes off with you hanging out of the side, your legs dangling in the air, you feel an awesome power. Chasing a powerful boat 30 ft. (9 m) above in a helicopter with the boat doing over 120 mph (193 kmh) is incredible.

Awesome Power

The twin Lamborghini V12 engines in the boat roar ferociously as the boat leaps out of the water. The helicopter blades contribute to the spine-tingling experience.

Film

You must choose the right type of film. The action is so fast paced, that your film needs to be a high speed too.

A powerboat in action.

Air riding with all four wheels, or the bottom of the board off the ground, short for aerial.

Backside a skateboarding trick or turn executed with the skater's back facing the ramp or obstacle.

BASE acronym for building, antennae, span, and earth. Jumping from a fixed object.

Boogie Board a board used to body surf. This is a great way to learn to surf.

Crampons irons attached to your boots used to help you climb on ice.

Face the front side of the wave.

Fakie the skater is in his or her normal stance, but the board is moving backwards.

Free Climbing a style of climbing that depends on the climber's footwork, ability, skill, and physical strength to pull him or her up the rock face.

Grind a boarding trick that scrapes one or both axles on a curb, railing, or other surface.

Halfpipe a U-shaped ramp of any size, usually with a flat section in the middle.

Hang Ten a surfing move where all ten of the surfer's toes are hanging off the front of the board. Usually done on a longboard.

Lift upward movement of air. Needed to keep kites, paragliders, and hang gliders aloft.

Ollie a jump where a boarder hops over obstacles, onto a curb, or other object.

Off-piste skiing or snowboarding in the backcountry. High risk of avalanche.

Ripping having your way with a wave.

Vert skating on ramps and other vertical structures, specifically designed for skating.

Vert Ramp a halfpipe, at least 8 ft. (2.5 m) tall, with steep sides that are perfectly vertical near the top.

Wipeout falling off the board.